Original title:
Crystal Glow

Copyright © 2024 Swan Charm
All rights reserved.

Author: Kene Elistrand
ISBN HARDBACK: 978-9916-79-576-7
ISBN PAPERBACK: 978-9916-79-577-4
ISBN EBOOK: 978-9916-79-578-1

Luminous Threads

In twilight's grasp, the threads align,
A tapestry of stars does shine.
Whispers dance on breezes light,
Stitching dreams through endless night.

Each glow a sign, a path to tread,
In hopes we weave, our hearts are fed.
With every turn, a story spun,
A journey bright, for everyone.

Radiant Echoes

The echoes call from valleys deep,
Where shadows fold, and secrets keep.
A laughter shared, in dusk's embrace,
Resonates through time and space.

Each word a spark, ignites the air,
Boundless warmth, a love to share.
In echoes pure, our voices blend,
A symphony that has no end.

Halo of Dreams

A halo glows around the night,
Bringing forth the softest light.
In every sigh and silent wish,
Flutters the heart, a gentle swish.

With every star, a hope takes flight,
In dreams we wander, hearts alight.
Through whispered paths, we find our way,
Guided by love, come what may.

Glimmers of Eternity

In fleeting moments, glimmers gleam,
A dance of time, a waking dream.
Each sparkle holds a tale untold,
Of fleeting warmth, of love so bold.

As seasons shift, our spirits soar,
Embracing life, forevermore.
In every breath, eternity sings,
Of joy and hope, the gift it brings.

Shiny Dreams

In the hush of the night, we soar,
Chasing whispers on wings, we explore.
Stars above twinkle, soft and bright,
Painting our hopes in silver light.

Clouds of wonder drift on by,
Weaving tales as they float high.
Each heartbeat syncs with the moon's glow,
In this realm where our wishes flow.

Through the roses of vibrant hue,
We gather moments, both old and new.
Lifting hearts, as we kindly bream,
In this world, we live our shiny dream.

Fingers touching the velvet sky,
With every thought, the dreams reply.
A dance of shadows, light will beam,
Guiding us forth in the gleam of dream.

As dawn approaches, colors blend,
In a canvas where dreams transcend.
With every step, the sun will gleam,
Forever bound in our shiny dream.

Cosmic Reflections

In the vastness where starlight plays,
I ponder on time and endless days.
Galaxies whisper secrets untold,
In their embrace, the universe holds.

Mirrors of light, where shadows dance,
Reflecting thoughts in a cosmic trance.
Nebulas swirl in a colorful stream,
Glinting softly like a waking dream.

Planets spin in a gentle sway,
Harmonizing with the Milky Way.
Each glimmer whispers a tale of old,
Of journeys woven in threads of gold.

With every glance at the night sky bright,
I'm lost in wonder, in pure delight.
Each star a wish, a fleeting spark,
Illuminating the velvet dark.

In this silence, I find my place,
Amongst the wonders of time and space.
Forever searching, in endless beams,
I lose myself in cosmic dreams.

Embedded in Light

In dawn's gentle embrace, we find,
The world awakens in colors combined.
Each ray of sun, a memory bright,
Whispers of love, embedded in light.

Shadows retreat as warmth takes hold,
Stories of warmth like whispers foretold.
Every glimmer, a promise made,
In the heart's garden, hopes are laid.

Through the trees, the sunlight weaves,
A tapestry rich with autumn leaves.
Dreams take shape, in brilliance they might,
Together we bask, embedded in light.

As twilight drapes its soft, dark cloak,
We gather dreams with every spoke.
In quiet moments, the heart ignites,
In the embrace of soft, golden sights.

Forever basking in fleeting beams,
Living our lives, pursuing our dreams.
In every heartbeat, the world ignites,
And love remains, embedded in light.

Ethereal Glints

In the realm where echoes play,
Ethereal glints guide the way.
Softly shimmering, the dreams arise,
Whispering secrets beneath bright skies.

Beneath the moon's tender gaze,
Waves of wonder in a hushed blaze.
Each twinkle weaves a fragile thread,
Binding the living with words unsaid.

As colors mingle in dusk's embrace,
Fleeting moments, a delicate trace.
Every heartbeat is an echoing dance,
In the shimmer, we find our chance.

Floating on whispers of starlit streams,
We embrace the beauty of fleeting dreams.
In twilight's embrace, we chase delight,
Brightening shadows with ethereal light.

Together we wander, hearts aligned,
In the glints of twilight, love confined.
Forever we wander through night's glints,
Chasing the beauty of ethereal hints.

Fractured Rainbows

Beneath the clouds, colors fade,
Splintered hues in sunlight laid.
Promises of joy, now blurred,
In silence, dreams are gently stirred.

Where laughter once danced in the air,
Echoes linger, a faint despair.
Shattered visions drift apart,
Yet hope persists within the heart.

Fragments of light on rainy days,
Glimpse of beauty, a fleeting gaze.
Though storms may come, and shadows rise,
Chasing the sun, we reach for skies.

Through the mist, a glimpse of grace,
A fractured rainbow finds its place.
In every drop, a story told,
A treasure in each shard of gold.

Veils of Stardust

Whispers of night in cosmic dance,
Veils of stardust, a fleeting chance.
Galaxies swirl in silent song,
A universe where dreams belong.

In shadows deep, a spark ignites,
Guiding hearts through endless nights.
Each twinkle, a wish on the breeze,
Binding souls with cosmic keys.

Mysterious paths, where echoes play,
Illuminate the night and day.
Veils unfold, revealing fate,
Awakening love, never too late.

In the depths, the infinite gleams,
We chase the constellations, our dreams.
Stardust whispers in gentle sighs,
A tapestry woven across the skies.

Gleaming Epiphany

In moments fleeting, clarity shows,
A seed of wisdom, a blossom grows.
Light breaks through the shadows of doubt,
Revealing truths we can't live without.

In quiet corners, thoughts collide,
Gleaming echoes where secrets hide.
The heart awakens, a gentle stir,
Each realization, a whispered blur.

Like morning dew on blades of grass,
Epiphanies shine, unable to mask.
Life's intricate dance in vibrant hues,
Guides us down the path we choose.

With every breath, we learn to see,
The beauty found in uncertainty.
In every doubt, a chance to grow,
A gleaming epiphany, aglow.

Luminous Fragments

Shattered mirrors on the ground,
In their pieces, light is found.
Each shard a story, a life once known,
Reflecting all that we've outgrown.

Through the cracks, the colors blend,
In chaos, beauty can ascend.
A tapestry of dreams undone,
Yet luminous hearts dance in the sun.

In the twilight, hope ignites,
Radiant whispers that soar to heights.
From fragments lost, we rise anew,
In every setback, a chance to pursue.

With open arms, we cherish the past,
In luminous fragments, freedom's cast.
Every tear and every smile,
Brings us back to our journey's style.

Resplendence of Being

In the glimmer of the dawn,
Where shadows dance and play,
Life awakens gently,
In hues of gold and gray.

The heart sings with rapture,
A melody so pure,
Each moment holds a treasure,
In love, we find the cure.

Joy spills like sunlight,
Filling the empty space,
Every breath a whisper,
In this sacred place.

With every fleeting heartbeat,
We cherish what's in sight,
The resplendence of being,
Shines through the darkest night.

Together we will wander,
Through valleys deep and wide,
In the warmth of each other,
Forever side by side.

Aurora's Lullaby

The soft glow of twilight,
Whispers secrets unheard,
As the sky turns pastel,
  Nature softly stirred.

Stars blink like diamonds,
In a velvet embrace,
Crickets hum their soft tune,
  Night's gentle lace.

Dreams drift like feathers,
On the cool evening breeze,
Wrapped in Aurora's warmth,
  Beneath swaying trees.

Each sigh is a story,
Told in silken sighs,
While the moonlight dances,
  In the boundless skies.

Close your eyes, dear wanderer,
Let the stars light your way,
In the arms of stillness,
  Find peace till break of day.

Celestial Radiance

In the stillness of night,
Dreams take flight on high,
Every star a promise,
Underneath the sky.

Whispers of the cosmos,
Echo soft and clear,
Guiding hearts to wonder,
While we linger near.

Galaxies unfolding,
In a dance so divine,
We find our place in starlight,
In the grand design.

With each pulse of starlight,
Our spirits intertwine,
Awakening the magic,
That makes us all align.

In celestial radiance,
We are never alone,
Bound by dreams and wishes,
In the universe's tone.

Twilight's Embrace

As daylight whispers goodbye,
In twilight's tender glow,
The world pauses to breathe,
And secrets begin to flow.

Colors blend and mingle,
In a soft watercolor hue,
Nature wraps in silence,
Awakening the new.

With shadows growing longer,
And stars peeking through,
The night wraps around us,
Like a blanket of dew.

Gentle breezes carry,
The hints of dusk's embrace,
A moment steeped in beauty,
In time's gentle grace.

In the hush of twilight,
We find solace and peace,
In the soft unfolding,
Where all worries cease.

Glimmering Horizons

Beneath the sky, a line so bright,
Waves whisper dreams in the soft twilight.
Shadows dance on the shimmering shore,
Hope's gentle pulse, forevermore.

Every star gleams with tales untold,
As night unfolds its blanket of gold.
The sun dips low, a fiery sigh,
Kindled wishes, ready to fly.

Silent moments stretch and bend,
With each heartbeat, worlds transcend.
In hues of purple, orange, and red,
A canvas where all dreams are fed.

Glimmers call from the far-off land,
Where futures blossom, just as planned.
Embrace the light; let worries cease,
In the glow, discover peace.

Facets of Serenity

In quiet whispers, the world unfolds,
Each moment cherished, like stories told.
Gentle breezes through branches glide,
Nature's lullaby, a soothing guide.

Clouds drift softly, in a sea of blue,
Encasing dreams in the clear, anew.
Cascades of laughter echo through air,
In serene spots, all burdens bare.

Moonlit nights bring a gentle balm,
Starlight quilted, ever calm.
Reflections shimmer on tranquil streams,
Navigating life through peaceful dreams.

Every heartbeat finds its tune,
In the cradle of dusk, beneath the moon.
A tapestry woven with threads of grace,
Facets of serenity, a warm embrace.

Dazzle in Twilight

As day sinks low, colors ignite,
The sky blazes crimson, pure delight.
Crisp air hums with a flavor sweet,
The dance of light on the evening street.

Shadows stretch and gently play,
Embracing secrets of the coming day.
Neon dreams in the fading light,
Glimpse of magic in the quiet night.

The stars awaken, one by one,
A gentle gaze at the setting sun.
Each twinkle sings of a tale to tell,
Dazzle unfolds, a mesmerizing spell.

Time slips by in a soft embrace,
Each fleeting moment wears its pace.
In twilight's glow, we find our way,
A bridge to dreams where hearts can sway.

Translucent Journey

On pathways paved with shadowed light,
We wander slowly, hearts in flight.
Each step taken paints the air,
With echoes of joy, love, and care.

Through forest trails and golden fields,
Nature whispers, the soul it yields.
With each sunrise, a fresh start blooms,
Hope unfurling from darkened tombs.

The mountains rise, steadfast and true,
Their peaks kissed softly by morning dew.
In every crest, we chase the dream,
Life's translucent path, a steady stream.

Rivers run deep, carrying grace,
Guiding us gently, a warm embrace.
In the journey's heart, we find our song,
Translucent tales where we belong.

Halos of Remembrance

In shadows deep, the memories stay,
Whispers of laughter, fading away.
Echoes of moments, sweet and bright,
Haloed in dreams, lost to the night.

Fading photographs, yellowed, worn,
Silent stories of love, gently torn.
Each glance a treasure, a time once shared,
In the heart's quiet, always prepared.

Candles flicker in the soft twilight,
Guiding lost souls towards the light.
With every tear, a connection remains,
Binding our hearts in joy and pain.

We hold on tight to what feels near,
Cherished remnants of those we hold dear.
In the fabric of time, we weave our thread,
Halos of remembrance, softly spread.

From ashes, wisdom, a gentle rise,
Through the veil, love never dies.
Forever cherished, always bright,
Halos gleam in the deepening night.

Sparkling Serenity

In tranquil waters, reflections dance,
Soft whispers carry, a sacred chance.
Stars above twinkle, a gentle hymn,
Inviting the heart to quietly swim.

Amidst the chaos, a still embrace,
Peaceful moments, a sacred space.
Breezes whisper through foliage green,
Nature's beauty, forever serene.

Each sunset paints the sky anew,
Crimson and gold in a calming view.
Time slows down, the world takes a pause,
In sparkling serenity, we find our cause.

With each heartbeat, the soul finds rest,
In the quiet, we're truly blessed.
Glimmers of peace in every sway,
Holding our worries gently at bay.

In the moments we cherish, we live free,
Finding solace by the gently sea.
Letting go, we fully embrace,
Sparkling serenity, a warm embrace.

Dream's Luster

In slumber's fold, where whispers roam,
Dreams take flight, a space called home.
Fleeting visions, soft and bright,
In the night sky, stars ignite.

Joyful colors in a world unseen,
Echoes of laughter, sweet and keen.
Chasing shadows, we dance and play,
In the arms of dreams, we drift away.

Each dream a portal, a wish ignites,
Radiant journeys on magical nights.
We taste the freedom, we grasp the light,
As creativity soars, taking flight.

In woven tales, we find our way,
Guided by starlight through the fray.
Awake or asleep, the heart's allure,
In dream's luster, we feel so pure.

With every dawn, a promise remains,
To follow the visions that spark in chains.
Dream's gentle laughter leads us along,
A melody sweet, a beautiful song.

Glimmer of the Infinite

In the vastness where horizons blend,
A glimmer shines, a journey's end.
Stars whisper secrets, old and wise,
Illuminating paths through the skies.

Every heartbeat echoes through the night,
A cosmic dance bathed in starlight.
Time unravels, a delicate thread,
Woven in dreams of the ones who've led.

Galaxies spinning, a celestial tune,
With each twinkle, we're drawn to the moon.
Every moment, a marvel to see,
In the glimmer, we set ourselves free.

In endless wonders, we find our grace,
Embracing the beauty in time and space.
With eyes wide open, we witness the birth,
Of infinity's glow, a priceless worth.

Connected forever, we dance with delight,
In the glimmer, we uncover the light.
Through trials and triumphs, we'll always strive,
For the glimmer of the infinite keeps us alive.

Twilight Gleam

The day descends, hues intertwine,
Stars awaken, their tales align.
Shadows dance in soft embrace,
Whispers linger, a gentle trace.

Beneath the arch of fading light,
Crickets sing, a sweet delight.
The sky blushes in purple hue,
Night's canvas, a dream anew.

Softly now the world does hush,
Moonlit paths in silver brush.
Each secret held in twilight's hold,
Stories woven, soft yet bold.

In this realm, the heart does soar,
Boundless wonders to explore.
Nature's lullaby gently calls,
In twilight's gleam, the magic sprawls.

Endless journeys seem so near,
In shadows deep, we lose our fear.
For in the dusk, all things may gleam,
Life unfolds like a dream's dream.

Glistening Pathways

Morning dew on emerald grass,
Footsteps soft as breezes pass.
Sunlight dances on the trail,
Nature's beauty, never stale.

Every turn a new surprise,
Beauty captured by the eyes.
Winding paths through ancient trees,
Whispers carried by the breeze.

Colors burst in vibrant hues,
Each step taken, life renews.
Glistening leaves in sunlight's thrall,
Nature's symphony, a call.

In every footprint, dreams reside,
Lessons learned, no need to hide.
Glistening pathways lead the way,
To endless adventures every day.

Beneath the sky, so vast and true,
Glistening paths for me and you.
Together we'll wander and roam,
Finding solace, making home.

Shining Whispers

In the silence, voices gleam,
Echoes of a fleeting dream.
Softly spoken, truths unwind,
Through the heart, they intertwine.

Shining whispers on the breeze,
Carried forth with gentle ease.
Secrets held in moonlit glow,
Guiding hearts where love may flow.

Tender words, a sacred song,
Binding souls, we've known so long.
In the twilight, shadows blend,
Whispers echo, love won't end.

Stars above us bear witness bright,
To the promises of the night.
In these moments, we ignite,
Shining whispers, pure delight.

Through the journey, hand in hand,
Together we will always stand.
In the quiet, love's embrace,
Shining whispers find their place.

Enigma of Radiance

In the night, a riddle glows,
Mysteries in shadows rose.
Light cascades, a gentle spark,
In the silence, whispers mark.

Flickering flames dance in the dark,
Each brushstroke a secret arc.
Radiance paints the sky anew,
Each hue speaks of stories true.

In the stillness, stars align,
Drawing hearts to the divine.
An enigma wrapped in light,
Paths illuminated bright.

Questions linger, answers hide,
In the glow where dreams abide.
Chasing shadows, we embrace,
The enigma, a timeless grace.

Guided by this glowing thread,
Through the maze where few have tread.
In every spark, a tale we find,
The enigma of radiance, intertwined.

Enchanted Luminescence

In the forest deep and wide,
Moonlight dances, shadows hide.
Whispers echo soft and clear,
Nature's pulse is drawing near.

Stars ignite the velvet sky,
Every twinkle, a sweet sigh.
Mysteries woven in the night,
Breath of magic, pure delight.

Trees adorned in silver glow,
Crickets sing their songs below.
Each leaf shines with secret dreams,
Awakened by the night's soft beams.

Winds unveil a gentle grace,
Time slows in this sacred space.
Heartbeats blend with song and light,
Life enchants the still of night.

As dawn breaks, the spell shall fade,
But memories never betrayed.
In the heart, it lingers still,
Enchanted by the night's sweet thrill.

Aurora of the Heart

Dawn awakens, colors swirl,
A canvas bright, emotions unfurl.
Soft pastels paint the waking skies,
A tender truth in morning's guise.

Golden rays caress the ground,
Hope, in whispers, can be found.
Each heartbeat sings a silent tune,
As flowers bloom beneath the moon.

The sun spills warmth like silken thread,
As shadows dance, the night's now shed.
Heart to heart, life intertwines,
A symphony in nature shines.

In every breath, a spark ignites,
A promise held in morning lights.
Through every trial, love remains,
The heart's aurora ever gains.

So let the dawn embrace your soul,
In light and love, we are made whole.
For every day brings fresh new start,
A golden glow, the aurora of the heart.

Silvery Veils

Fog drapes softly on the ground,
Secrets hidden all around.
Whispers linger in the air,
Silvery veils beyond compare.

Moonbeams weave through branches low,
Casting shadows, soft aglow.
Night unwraps its silken shroud,
Unveiling dreams, both clear and loud.

Echoes of the past resound,
In this realm, magic is found.
Each sigh carried on the breeze,
Wave of wonder, hearts to tease.

Time dissolves in misty grace,
Lost within this timeless space.
Underneath the shimmering gleam,
We awaken from the dream.

As dawn arrives, the veils retreat,
Yet memories remain so sweet.
Silvery threads of night once spun,
Bind us gently, two as one.

Light's Embrace

In the garden, shadows play,
Morning light greets the day.
Petals open, colors bloom,
In the warmth, we shed our gloom.

Every ray, a soft caress,
Filling hearts with tenderness.
Nature's song, a sweet refrain,
In light's embrace, we break the chain.

Sunlight dances on the leaves,
Bringing forth what heart believes.
Glistening drops on grass so bright,
Each a gem in morning's light.

We find solace in the glow,
Wherever life may ebb and flow.
In the warmth, we feel the grace,
Forever held in light's embrace.

So let us cherish every spark,
In the light, we leave our mark.
Together in this radiant space,
We are one in light's embrace.

Shining Shadows

In the twilight's gentle embrace,
Whispers dance with the light.
Silent secrets intertwine,
Casting shadows into the night.

Stars shimmer like hidden gems,
Glistening in the dark sky.
They reveal the stories lost,
Of a time long gone by.

Footprints trace a forgotten path,
Where dreams and shadows merge.
A beckoning call from the past,
With every breath, we surge.

With each heartbeat, a promise made,
To cherish every tone.
In these shining shadows,
We find our way back home.

Musical Luminescence

Notes float in the evening air,
Like glowing fireflies in flight.
Each melody a soft caress,
A symphony of pure delight.

Strings tremble with whispered dreams,
As the moonlight shines bright.
Echoes of love gently linger,
In the depth of the night.

Rhythms pulse like a heartbeat,
Creating a dance of the soul.
In this musical luminescence,
We find ourselves whole.

Harmony and grace entwined,
In every note that we play.
A celebration of our spirits,
In this luminous ballet.

Halo of Dreams

In the quiet of the night,
A halo of dreams appears.
Soft whispers fill the air,
Chasing away all fears.

Fragments of light intertwine,
With hopes yet to be found.
Each one glimmers with promise,
In this enchanted ground.

Clouds drift beneath the stars,
Casting shadows of delight.
Together we wander gently,
Under the silvery light.

With every thought, we soar high,
Into realms yet to explore.
In this halo of dreams,
Our spirits start to roar.

Spectral Journeys

Beyond the veil of time's own face,
We embark on spectral journeys.
Where echoes of the past still shine,
And mysteries linger in deep sturnies.

Colors blend in a vibrant dance,
Painting tales upon the breeze.
Spectres weave through forgotten paths,
With grace and silent ease.

Every step is an unfolding,
Of truth wrapped in twilight's grace.
We chase the shadows of yesterdays,
In this ethereal space.

Cascading dreams lead the way,
To realms unseen by the eye.
In these spectral journeys,
Our spirits learn to fly.

Glisten of the Soul

In twilight's gentle glow, we find,
A whispering breeze, soft and kind.
Stars emerge, like dreams untold,
Glimmers of hope, in night's hold.

A heart beats softly in the dark,
Each pulse a note, a fleeting spark.
Echoes of love, floating around,
In the silence, beauty is found.

Raindrops dance on a window pane,
Each one a story, a soft refrain.
In the stillness, joy and pain,
Glisten like stars, sweetly remain.

Moments captured, like fireflies,
Flickering softly, where memory lies.
The soul's journey, through shadows cast,
In fleeting glances, shadows pass.

Awake we rise with each new dawn,
With every breath, a chance is drawn.
In the morning light, fears unfold,
The glisten of life, a joy retold.

Shimmering Heartstrings

In twilight's hold, heartstrings gleam,
A tapestry woven of tender dreams.
Each thread whispers, secrets shared,
In the dance of love, souls bared.

Gentle echoes, a soft embrace,
In the silence, we find our place.
Notes of laughter, tears that flow,
Shimmering heartstrings, ever aglow.

Moments linger, like fragrant blooms,
In twilight's hush, the past resumes.
Connections forged in whispered words,
In the symphony of love, we're heard.

Together we weave, through night and day,
A melody bright, come what may.
In the stillness, we intertwine,
Shimmering heartstrings, forever shine.

As dawn breaks, new hopes arise,
In morning's light, our spirits soar high.
In every heartbeat, love will sing,
Shimmering heartstrings, the joy you bring.

Rays of Tranquility

In quiet moments, rays extend,
Through gentle whispers, the heart will mend.
A serene light, soft and warm,
Guides us gently, through the storm.

Each breath a gift, peace we embrace,
Nature's beauty, a sacred space.
Calming waves upon the shore,
Rays of tranquility, forevermore.

Stars that twinkle, soothing sight,
In the stillness, they bring light.
Night's deep veil, a resting place,
Wrapped in dreams, we find our grace.

In morning's glow, we rise anew,
With every dawn, fresh dreams to pursue.
As sunlight pours, fears dissipate,
Rays of tranquility illuminate.

With every heartbeat, a still refrain,
In the dance of life, we find our chain.
Bound together, 'neath skies so blue,
Rays of tranquility, ever true.

Warmth of the Dawn

As darkness fades, the day will wake,
A tender light, for love's sweet sake.
Golden hues that kiss the morn,
The warmth of the dawn, where hope is born.

In every gesture, gentleness lies,
With open hearts, we touch the skies.
Whispers of promise in the air,
In the warmth of the dawn, we share.

Buds of spring in softest bloom,
Carried along by morning's plume.
In laughter and joy, the memories play,
When dawn arrives, it lights our way.

Embrace the light as shadows flee,
In radiant warmth, we are set free.
Each moment a treasure, love's bright spawn,
A symphony sweet, the warmth of dawn.

As day unfolds, we take our stand,
Hand in hand, we trace this land.
With every sunrise, our spirits drawn,
Together forever, in the warmth of dawn.

Ethereal Twilight

In whispers soft the shadows play,
As daylight bows to dusk's ballet.
Stars awaken in velvet skies,
While the moon unfolds her silver guise.

A gentle breeze begins to sigh,
Carrying dreams that drift and fly.
Colors blend in twilight's grace,
Painting peace upon each face.

The night reveals a tranquil scene,
Where starlight dances, pure and clean.
A tranquil heart finds comfort here,
In the hush where all is clear.

Crickets serenade the night,
Nature's song, a soft delight.
In the twilight's gentle hands,
Ethereal whispers take their stands.

As the world slips into rest,
In quietude, we feel the best.
The night unfolds a velvet scroll,
An ethereal dream for every soul.

Prisms of the Soul

Within the heart, a light does gleam,
Reflecting hopes, a radiant dream.
Colors swirl in vibrant dance,
A kaleidoscope of chance.

Shadows fade as light takes flight,
Transforming darkness into bright.
Every hue a story told,
In prisms bright, our truths unfold.

Through every tear, a rainbow shows,
In the depth of pain, beauty grows.
Fragments pieced with tender care,
Each facet shines, a love laid bare.

In the stillness, whispers sing,
Echoes of what the heart can bring.
From shattered shards, a vision whole,
Painting life with prisms of the soul.

A tapestry of light and shade,
In every step, a path is laid.
Through the mirror, bright and bold,
We find ourselves in stories told.

Sparkling Whimsy

In a world of dreams, we twirl and spin,
Chasing giggles where joys begin.
Bubbles rise with laughter's sound,
A sparkling whimsy all around.

Frolicking through fields of gold,
Stories whispered, laughter told.
We dance beneath the sunlit skies,
Where every child's imagination flies.

A sprinkle of magic in every heart,
Joyous laughter, a work of art.
With twinkling eyes and joyful gaze,
We embrace life's whimsical maze.

In gentle breezes, whispers play,
Turning moments into a ballet.
Each sparkle shines, a fleeting glance,
Inviting us to join the dance.

So let us revel in whims so bright,
Where dreams take wing in endless flight.
Together we'll weave the tales unspun,
In a world of sparkle, we are one.

Radiance Unseen

In the quiet hush of dawn's embrace,
Lives a beauty, a hidden grace.
Though sometimes shrouded, it brightly gleams,
A radiance woven through our dreams.

Beneath the surface, light ignites,
Illuminating shadowed nights.
Tender thoughts in silence bloom,
Filling hearts and chasing gloom.

With every heartbeat, hope does rise,
A whispered truth beneath the skies.
In the depths of our soul's unseen,
We find the light that forever beams.

Like stars that twinkle in the dark,
Gathered dreams ignite a spark.
Reflecting love in every scene,
Illuminating paths, a radiance unseen.

So hold the light that lives within,
Let it guide where you begin.
For in each shadow, truth can shine,
A journey where our hearts align.

Glowing Reverberations

In the hush of twilight's grace,
Whispers dance through the place.
Softly glowing, shadows intertwine,
Reverberations of the divine.

Colors ripple, gentle and bright,
Each pulse a spark, igniting the night.
The heart feels the rhythm, a tender embrace,
In glowing whispers, we find our space.

Stars twinkle, a heavenly choir,
Echoing hopes, setting dreams on fire.
Every flicker tells a tale untold,
In glowing reverberations, we are bold.

Moonlight bathes the world in gold,
A magic scene, warm and old.
Each heartbeat syncs with the cosmic sway,
In glowing reverberations, we drift away.

Transcend the silence, let your soul wander,
In the glow of reverberations, we ponder.
Connected to whispers, we softly sway,
In harmony with the night, we stay.

Dazzling Rhapsody

A melody rises with the dawn,
Each note a weapon, a graceful brawn.
Colors collide in a vibrant swirl,
Dazzling rhythms unfurl.

Joy spills forth from every key,
As the heart beats wild and free.
Strings resonate with a luscious sound,
In this rhapsody, we are found.

Light fractures, creating rainbows bright,
Compositions that ignite the night.
In unity, a symphony of dreams,
Dazzling rhapsody, bursting at the seams.

Voices lift like a gentle breeze,
Carried away with effortless ease.
Together we weave a tale so grand,
In this dazzling rhapsody, we stand.

Every heartbeat marks a chord,
Echoes of love in this accord.
Euphony rises, lifting the veil,
In dazzling rhapsody, we prevail.

Light's Cascade

A river of radiance flows near,
Whispers of clarity, bright and clear.
In every droplet, a spark of grace,
Light's cascade in an endless chase.

The horizon glows with a warm embrace,
A dance of shadows, a sacred space.
With each ripple, we find our way,
In light's cascade, welcoming the day.

Sunbeams shower like golden rain,
Washing away the remnants of pain.
In this cascade, we're reborn anew,
With every glimmer, we see what's true.

Colors merge, a painter's delight,
In the embrace of shimmering light.
We surrender to the luminous flow,
In light's cascade, let your soul glow.

Beyond the veil, where the spirit sings,
In harmony with the universe, it brings.
A gentle reminder of beauty's parade,
In the wonder of light's cascade.

Effulgent Echo

In the depths of silence, we find a spark,
Effulgent echoes that ignite the dark.
Resonance flows like a river wide,
In every heartbeat, a shimmering tide.

Voices rise, an ethereal tune,
Dancing softly beneath the moon.
With each note, our souls align,
In effulgent echoes, love will shine.

Magnificence wrapped in gentle sound,
In every layer, beauty is found.
Whispers of dreams linger in the air,
In effulgent echoes, we boldly dare.

Each shimmer a story, a tale to share,
As hearts entwine in the astral care.
Through time and space, our spirits soar,
In effulgent echoes, forevermore.

Timeless resonance, a cosmic embrace,
In the theater of stars, we find our place.
Synchronized with the universe's flow,
In the magic of effulgent echo.

Beacons of Hope

In the distance, flames arise,
Guiding souls through darkened skies.
A whisper of dreams, softly spoken,
Promises held, yet unbroken.

Stars above, a shimmering light,
Leading hearts in the still night.
Through shadows deep, we find our way,
Trusting the dawn of a new day.

In storms of doubt, a steady glow,
Reminding us, we're not alone.
Hands joined together, fear dismissed,
With every step, we persist.

The echoes of laughter fill the breeze,
Carried by hope, our hearts at ease.
For every struggle, there's a chance,
To rise again, to learn, to dance.

Together we stand, the future bright,
Chasing shadows, embracing light.
With beacons of hope, we'll never tire,
Our spirits soar, fueled by fire.

Celestial Gleam

Above the clouds, a soft blue hue,
Galaxies whisper secrets true.
The moonlight dances on tranquil seas,
In cosmic warmth, our spirits ease.

Nebulas bloom like flowers in spring,
Each star a note in the song they sing.
Time bends gently, a tapestry spun,
In the arms of the night, we are one.

Infinity calls with a gentle sigh,
Through velvet skies, our dreams can fly.
In shimmering glints, our hopes ascend,
Beneath celestial wonders, hearts mend.

Waves of light pulse through the dark,
Illuminating paths, igniting a spark.
We reach for the heights, arms open wide,
As the universe breathes, we glide.

With each dawn, a memory is made,
In the dance of stars, we are not afraid.
For in this vast realm, we amaze,
Caught in the glimmer of cosmic gaze.

Iridescent Tides

The ocean whispers secrets old,
With every wave, a tale retold.
A dance of colors beneath the sun,
As tides converge, spirits run.

Each crest a dream, each trough a sigh,
In harmony's rhythm, we learn to fly.
With iridescent hues, the waters gleam,
Carrying hope in every stream.

The shores embrace our fleeting thoughts,
In every ripple, a memory caught.
Footprints wash away, but still we feel,
The strength of the tides, a gentle heal.

Shells hidden deep, treasures await,
Messages of love, our fates create.
As we gather pearls from the sands of time,
We find our voices in whispered rhyme.

Forever changing, the sea will sing,
Of endless journeys, the joy they bring.
In iridescent tides, we lose and find,
The beauty of life, in heart and mind.

Illuminated Secrets

In shadows cast, the light reveals,
Hidden truths and tender feels.
Moments captured, softly bright,
Illuminated secrets of the night.

With lanterns held, we search for grace,
Exploring depths of time and space.
Every heartbeat, a story to tell,
In whispers of twilight, a magic spell.

Through twisted paths, the glow invites,
To discover dreams in starry nights.
Mysteries dance on the edge of sight,
In silence profound, we find our light.

Flickering flames, a promise shared,
Trusting the journey, though we are scared.
With each revelation, our spirits grow,
In illuminated secrets, we'll always know.

As dawn approaches, shadows fade,
But within our hearts, the light's parade.
Every secret softly gleaned,
Becomes a tapestry, brightly dreamed.

Aurora's Embrace

In dawn's soft glow, the world awakes,
Colors dance, a canvas breaks.
Whispers of light, in the sky they twirl,
A dream unfolds, as night starts to unfurl.

Beneath the arch of morning's breath,
Nature sings, defying death.
Golden rays on dew-kissed grass,
Moments held, too sweet to pass.

Mountains blush with rosy hue,
A silent promise, fresh and new.
Waves of warmth in the crisp air,
Wrapped in love, without a care.

Echoes of laughter fill the space,
As shadows run from light's embrace.
In this hour, we find our way,
Dancing, dreaming, come what may.

Hand in hand, through every rise,
We chase the sun across the skies.
In Aurora's arms, we find our place,
Together woven, in time and space.

Incandescent Heart

In twilight's glow, a spark ignites,
Filling the void; casting delights.
Whispers of flame, in shadows dance,
Capturing souls in a fervent trance.

Moments linger, bright and rare,
Every heartbeat, a silent prayer.
In the stillness, where feelings collide,
Love's incandescent glow cannot hide.

Embers flicker with hopes unspoken,
In the silence, connections woven.
Through the night, our spirits soar,
In the light, we will explore.

Chasing dreams like shooting stars,
Illuminating the path, free of scars.
Hold on tight, let fears depart,
Forever bound, an incandescent heart.

In each glance, a universe found,
Two kindred souls, forever unbound.
Let love's fire burn bright and true,
In this dance, it's me and you.

Light Between Shadows

In the depth of night, shadows creep,
Yet a glimmer of hope starts to seep.
Softly glowing, a path appears,
Guiding us through our hidden fears.

In whispers of wind, a tale unfolds,
Of bravery, courage, and hearts of gold.
Light cuts through the darkest places,
Illuminating forgotten faces.

With every step, the burden fades,
As luminescence gently cascades.
The dance of light, a sacred bond,
In the silence, we learn to respond.

Through trials faced, we find our way,
In the quiet moments, we choose to stay.
Holding tight to the flickering flame,
Knowing well we're never the same.

Together we rise, hand in hand,
Chasing the dream, making a stand.
In the light between shadows, we thrive,
With love as our beacon, we come alive.

Reflections in the Mist

In the early morn, when silence reigns,
Mist hangs low, like whispered chains.
Mirrored waters, secrets confined,
In every ripple, a truth we find.

Branches beckon, cloaked in grey,
Nature's artwork, on bright display.
Each droplet gleams, a fleeting glance,
In the stillness, we take a chance.

A world transformed, in soft embrace,
Dreams take shape, a tender grace.
With every gaze, a story flows,
In reflections, the heart only knows.

Breathe in deeply, let thoughts take flight,
Through veils of fog, we seek the light.
In the dance of haze, we learn to trust,
Finding beauty in the subtle gust.

As day unfolds, the mists retreat,
Revealing wonders, bittersweet.
In every moment, a whisper persists,
An echo of love, in reflections we missed.

Prism Dance

Colors swirl in the light,
As shadows weave through the night.
They twirl in a vibrant embrace,
Creating a joyous space.

Every hue finds its place,
In this harmonious chase.
Echoes of laughter ignite,
In the heart of delight.

Soft whispers of the breeze,
Caress the dancing trees.
Nature joins in the song,
Where our spirits belong.

In a world spun anew,
Of red, green, and blue.
Infinite moments to share,
In this prism affair.

As dusk turns to dawn,
And the colors are drawn.
We join hands in a trance,
To a timeless prism dance.

Veil of Tranquility

Beneath a sky painted gray,
The worries slowly sway.
Wrapped in a gentle sigh,
We find peace as we lie.

Soft echoes of the streams,
Carry with them our dreams.
Time pauses in embrace,
As we drift in this space.

Leaves rustle with the breeze,
Whispers float like teasing tease.
In this calm, we forget,
Any lingering regret.

The world fades far away,
As twilight steals the day.
Wrapped in nature's shawl,
Tranquility, our all.

In silence, our hearts bloom,
Lighting up the dark room.
Hand in hand, here we stand,
In the calm of the land.

Moonlit Glimmer

Under the silver crest,
The night wears its best.
Stars twinkle from afar,
Guiding dreams like a star.

Whispers of the moonlight,
Wrap the world in pure white.
Soft shadows begin to play,
In the heart of the day.

A dance of light and dark,
Leaves a gentle mark.
Every moment feels rare,
A treasure we all share.

Ripples across the lake,
Reflect the paths we take.
In this glimmer, we find,
The magic intertwined.

As night surrenders to dawn,
New memories are drawn.
In the glow of the light,
We embrace the pure night.

Shimmering Paths

Through fields of gleaming light,
We wander, hearts in flight.
Every step leads us on,
To a world reborn.

Petals dance with the breeze,
Whispers carried with ease.
In the sunlight's warm grasp,
We find joy in the clasp.

Footprints weave through the grass,
Each moment, a chance to pass.
Nature's map, vast and true,
Guiding me back to you.

As shadows stretch and fade,
In the sunlight, we're made.
With hands held side by side,
We traverse the bright tide.

Through shimmering fields we tread,
Where dreams and love are bred.
In this dance of our lives,
The shimmering path thrives.

Ethereal Glow

In twilight's embrace, the stars ignite,
A whisper of dreams takes to flight.
Moonbeams dance on soft, serene waves,
Cradling the night as time gently paves.

Petals unfold in silvered dew,
A melody hums, pure and true.
The cosmos sighs a fragrant tune,
As skies unveil their emerald rune.

Veils of mist in the cool night's air,
Seal secrets wrapped with tender care.
The world slows down in a silken glow,
Where shadows shimmer and spirits flow.

Spiral of Lumens

In a dance of lights, the colors weave,
A tapestry bright, of dreams we achieve.
Each flicker shines with purpose and grace,
Inviting the heart to find its place.

Waves of warmth, through cosmos spread,
Illuminate paths where dreams are led.
Each shimmered star tells stories bold,
Of journeys sought and treasures told.

Through spirals of lumens, we twirl and spin,
Hand in hand, new worlds begin.
In radiance strong, our hopes arise,
Filling the voids with endless skies.

Opalescent Veils

Veils that shimmer, soft and bright,
Whisper secrets of the night.
Colors mingle in gentle swirls,
Crafting dreams, where magic unfurls.

In every glimmer, a story unfolds,
Of timeless journeys and hearts of gold.
Woven gently by the loom of fate,
Embracing the beauty, never too late.

As we wander through each opal hue,
The fabric of life speaks true and new.
In silence, we learn to understand,
The language of souls, hand in hand.

Reflections of the Heart

In the still waters, truths reflect,
A quiet gaze, where paths intersect.
Each ripple whispers tales untold,
Of love and loss, both fragile and bold.

Through the glassy sheen, memories glide,
Moments cherished, with arms open wide.
Each heartbeat echoes, softly it sings,
A symphony of hope that the heart brings.

In reflections deep, we find our way,
With courage as light, we shall not sway.
Together we face what life does impart,
In every glance, reflections of the heart.

Chasing Radiance

In the dawn of a hopeful day,
Shadows fade and dreams take flight.
Colors dance with vibrant play,
Chasing rays of purest light.

Whispers of the morning breeze,
Carry warmth on gentle wings.
Nature's song, a soothing tease,
Refrain of joy that life brings.

Mountains stand, majestic, proud,
Guardians of the skies above.
Through the mist, across the crowd,
We pursue what we all love.

With each step, our hopes align,
Paths entwined with golden thread.
In the distance, dreams will shine,
Radiance where our hearts are led.

Together toward the endless gleam,
Onward, brave, we rise and strive.
In this journey, we will dream,
Chasing radiance, we thrive.

Twilight Refraction

As the sun dips low and sighs,
The world bathes in a soft hue.
Stars awaken in the skies,
Reflections dance in vibrant view.

Through the twilight's gentle touch,
Shadows blend and merge as one.
In this hour, it means so much,
Moments held till day is done.

Whispers weave among the trees,
Nature's heart begins to glow.
Carried on a cool night breeze,
Magic stirs, and dreams will flow.

Each shimmering light, our guide,
Leading us through night's embrace.
In the quiet, we confide,
Finding solace in this space.

As the moon begins to rise,
Hope refracts in silver streams.
In the dark, our spirits fly,
Twilight holds our deepest dreams.

Luster of Time

In the folds of yesterday,
Memories gleam like polished stone.
Each moment holds its own bouquet,
The luster of time, softly shone.

Youthful laughter, distant calls,
Echoes of a world we knew.
Life's rich canvas, bright or small,
Brushstrokes bold and whispers true.

Seasons turn, the heart grows wise,
Leaves of gold in autumn fall.
Through the years, we learn to rise,
Finding beauty in it all.

Golden threads weave tales of old,
Stories cherished, tales retold.
In our hearts, their warmth we hold,
Shimmering with a dance of gold.

The luster of time forever shines,
In every laugh and tear we find.
Moments crafted like fine designs,
Treasured pieces, forever entwined.

Glimmering Horizons

At the edge where the sea meets sky,
Glimmers spark the morning's breath.
Waves of light, a soft goodbye,
Promises of life, not death.

On the horizon, dreams take flight,
Chasing echoes of the past.
Every shadow, every light,
Kisses of time, fleeting but vast.

Clouds like whispers, tales unfold,
Stories of those brave and bold.
In their shimmer, truths hold tight,
Guiding wayfarers through the night.

With each dawn, horizons glow,
New beginnings, paths to chase.
In this glimmer, we all know,
Hope resides in every place.

Together hand in hand we stride,
Into the dawn's embrace, we roam.
In the glimmering, we'll confide,
Horizons promise us a home.

Radiant Shards

In the dawn's embrace, light spills forth,
Fragmented gems upon the earth.
Each shard a story, sweetly told,
In colors bright, in hues of gold.

Dancing softly on the breeze,
Echoing laughter through the trees.
Shimmering dreams beneath the sky,
A tapestry woven, you and I.

With every twinkle, hope shall rise,
Reflecting love in evanescent skies.
Guided by stars in the velvet night,
Together we shine, forever bright.

Whispers of joy, hearts intertwined,
In every glimmer, solace we find.
Radiant shards, our spirits merge,
In the quiet moments, passions surge.

The world awakens, painted anew,
With radiant hues in every view.
As daylight fades, our dreams take flight,
In the comforting arms of the night.

Luminous Whispers

In twilight's hush, whispers ignite,
Words carried softly, a guiding light.
Luminous echoes of love's sweet song,
Through shadows and silence, we both belong.

Beneath the stars, secrets unfold,
Stories of futures yet to be told.
A dance of shadows, a flicker of grace,
In each gentle breath, we find our place.

Moonlit pathways, stepping so slow,
With every heartbeat, our spirits glow.
Luminous whispers guide our way,
Filling the night with a tender sway.

Voices entwined in the softest breeze,
Cradled in moments, hearts at ease.
The melody lingers, a sweet soft sigh,
In luminous whispers, just you and I.

As dawn approaches, our dreams align,
With each fleeting shadow, our souls entwine.
In the light of morning, we'll rise and shine,
Forever together, your hand in mine.

Gleaming Visions

In the mist of dreams, visions arise,
Gleaming reflections beneath the skies.
Colors swirl in a cosmic dance,
Inviting hearts to take a chance.

Whispers of fate weave through the air,
Painting hope with a vibrant flair.
In every shimmer, possibilities bloom,
A garden of wishes in gentle spring's gloom.

The dawn reveals what the night concealed,
Gleaming visions in light revealed.
With open hearts, we'll chart the way,
Guided by dreams that refuse to sway.

Together we'll sail on the wings of bliss,
In every moment, find our sweet kiss.
Gleaming visions, forever we chase,
In the canvas of time, we find our place.

As stars fade softly into the morn,
With newfound strength, we shall be reborn.
Embracing the day with laughter and cheer,
In gleaming visions, love is always near.

Ethereal Gleam

In the quiet night, a soft ethereal gleam,
Whispers of magic, drifting like a dream.
Stars twinkle above in celestial flow,
Guiding our hearts where love can grow.

With every pulse, the universe sings,
Inviting us softly to spread our wings.
Ethereal treasures in the depths of soul,
A radiant journey to make us whole.

In the stillness, we'll forge our fate,
Turning each moment to something great.
The gleam of the heart, forever bright,
Shining through darkness, a beacon of light.

Together we wander, hand in hand,
In a world painted by our own command.
With ethereal gleam, we shall ignite,
A fire of passion that soars in flight.

As dawn paints the horizon blue,
Ethereal moments lead us anew.
In the beauty of now, we'll forever stay,
With love as our guide, lighting the way.

Vivid Reverie

In depths of night, dreams take flight,
Colors dance in quiet delight.
Whispers echo through the mind,
Lost in shadows, treasures find.

The stars weave tales in silver streams,
Casting visions, woven dreams.
A world where fantasy holds sway,
In vivid hues, we drift away.

With each heartbeat, reality bends,
Time dissolves; the journey transcends.
Through lush meadows and ancient trees,
We wander freely on gentle breeze.

In twilight's embrace, thoughts unfurl,
A magical realm, a sparkling swirl.
Each moment holds a secret song,
In vivid reverie, we belong.

As dawn breaks softly, dreams take pause,
Though fleeting now, we give them applause.
For in our hearts, they linger still,
A vivid reverie, a cherished thrill.

Flicker of Joy

In the morning light, hearts awake,
Moments of bliss are ours to take.
A gentle smile, a kind gesture,
Life's simple gifts, our greatest treasure.

With laughter ringing, spirits lift,
In shared moments, we find our gift.
Each fleeting second, a reason to play,
A flicker of joy brightens the day.

Through storms and shadows, we weave our way,
Finding solace in love's bright ray.
Holding close those we cherish most,
In warmth of friendship, we proudly boast.

Waves of happiness crash and recede,
In little glimmers, we plant each seed.
With a twinkle in our eyes, we glow,
A flicker of joy, forever flows.

As twilight rolls in, and stars appear,
We gather our blessings, year after year.
For in every heartbeat, pure love will lay,
A flicker of joy, lighting the way.

Illuminated Pathways

Beneath the moon's soft, silvery light,
We wander forth into the night.
With every step, the path unfolds,
In illuminated dreams, life is told.

Through gardens lush and skies so wide,
We seek the truth, with hearts our guide.
Each twist and turn, a lesson learned,
With every spark, our spirits burned.

Branches sway and softly sigh,
Carrying whispers of the sky.
In nature's lap, we find our way,
Along illuminated pathways play.

When shadows rise and doubts appear,
Trust the light that's always near.
With courage found in love's embrace,
We journey forth, and time we chase.

As morning breaks and dawn is born,
A brighter world we greet with scorn.
For all we've traveled, love stays true,
On illuminated pathways, I walk with you.

Glowing Threads

In the tapestry of life, we weave,
Threads of color, never to leave.
Each strand a story, bright and bold,
In glowing patterns, our lives unfold.

With laughter stitched into the seams,
And love embroidered in our dreams.
Each moment treasured, never to fray,
In glowing threads, we find our way.

Through trials faced and mountains climbed,
In every heartbeat, we are primed.
To embrace the beauty, the light in strife,
In glowing threads, we stitch our life.

As nights grow cold and shadows near,
Hold tight the warmth that draws us near.
For every thread, a bond unique,
In glowing threads, our hearts shall speak.

So let us gather, hand in hand,
In this grand weave, together we stand.
With every stitch, a legacy spreads,
In love and laughter, glowing threads.

Light's Gentle Caress

In the dawn, the warmth awakes,
Caressing fields where silence breaks.
Whispers soft, a calming breeze,
Kissing petals on the trees.

A golden touch on dew-kissed grass,
Moments fleeting, shadows pass.
Hope ignites with each soft ray,
Guiding hearts through night to day.

Gentle gleams on water's face,
Nature's love in sweet embrace.
Every shimmer tells a tale,
Of life's journey, soft and frail.

As twilight draws its velvet dome,
Stars ignite, a skyward home.
Embers glow in fading light,
A promise held through darkest night.

In every gleam, a story spun,
With every ray, our souls are one.
Light's gentle touch forever stays,
Illuminating endless ways.

Lustrous Whisper

In the hush of moonlit nights,
Secrets dance in silver lights.
A gentle breeze, a lover's sigh,
Echoes soft as stars drift by.

Whispers weave through fragrant air,
Promises made, a silent prayer.
Hearts entwined as shadows play,
In the warmth, we lose the day.

Every glance, a spark ignites,
Illumined dreams in whispered flights.
Fingers trace the path we chase,
In this hush, we find our place.

Beyond the dawn's embrace anew,
With every heartbeat, love rings true.
In the glow where wishes dwell,
A lustrous tale, our secret spell.

Together bound through time's soft hand,
In this space, forever stand.
Whispers echo in the dark,
A love song's soft, eternal spark.

Radiance of the Soul

Glowing bright within the heart,
Every beat, a work of art.
Illumined paths we slowly tread,
With every thought, the light is fed.

In every dawn, new chances bloom,
Dispelling shadows, chasing gloom.
Radiant dreams take flight and soar,
Opening wide each hidden door.

A beacon bright in stormy skies,
In darkest hours, the spirit flies.
With every tear, a lesson learned,
Through every loss, our passions burned.

Unity in every glow,
A warmth that only lovers know.
Together shining, side by side,
In the radiance, we confide.

Embrace the light that life bestows,
With open hearts, the magic grows.
In the depths of our soul's light,
We find our peace, our guiding night.

Shimmering Dreams

Caught in realms where wishes dance,
Dreams unfold in sweet romance.
Lightly drifting through the night,
Casting shadows, soft and bright.

Colors swirl in twilight's hue,
Shimmering paths where hopes flow through.
Every secret softly gleams,
Painting skies with vibrant dreams.

In the silence, visions play,
Guiding souls along the way.
With each sparkle, visions call,
In this realm, we have it all.

The night whispers of what can be,
In shimmering hues, we dance carefree.
Stars align to grant a glance,
As dreams awaken in a trance.

Awake in dreams where magic lies,
Underneath those timeless skies.
With every breath, we chase the light,
In shimmering dreams, we find our flight.

Spectrum of Introspection

In colors deep, my mind does roam,
Thoughts like shadows, finding home.
Each hue a tale, unspooled and bare,
A canvas bright, emotions flare.

Reflections dance on thoughts I weave,
In silent whispers, I believe.
Each shade a truth, a hidden key,
Unlocking doors, setting me free.

In quiet corners of my soul,
A spectrum speaks, it makes me whole.
With every glance, the colors twist,
A vibrant world, too bright to miss.

The journey bends through time and space,
With every shade, I find my place.
In shades of dark, in shades of light,
I learn to soar, I learn to fight.

So let me wander, let me dream,
In every color, feel the gleam.
For in this spectrum, I will find,
The many layers of my mind.

Glistening Melodies

Soft notes rise with morning light,
Songs of joy take graceful flight.
Each chord a breath, a heartbeat true,
Whispers sweet, from me to you.

The rhythm flows like gentle streams,
Carrying hopes, and fragile dreams.
In every pause, a moment waits,
Melodies sweet, love resonates.

Together we'll dance, in perfect tune,
Underneath a shining moon.
With every harmony, hearts entwine,
In this music, our souls align.

The world's a stage, where we belong,
In every silence, a hidden song.
Let laughter echo, let voices blend,
In glistening notes, our hearts ascend.

So let us sing, let us believe,
In every note, we can achieve.
Together we'll weave a tapestry,
A symphony of you and me.

Light's Whispering Embrace

Through golden rays, the sunlight streams,
A tender touch that softly gleams.
In every beam, a story told,
Of warmth and hope, worth more than gold.

With gentle hands, it cradles night,
Transforming darkness into light.
In shadows cast, a glimmer shines,
As dreams emerge in fragile lines.

The morning dew, a shimmering lace,
Each drop reflects a sacred space.
In whispered tones, it calls to me,
To find the beauty, to just be free.

As sunlight fades, the stars ignite,
A tender dance of day and night.
In every flicker, I find my way,
In light's embrace, I long to stay.

So let me walk where light will lead,
In every moment, I am freed.
For in this glow, I find my peace,
In light's embrace, my soul's release.

Harmonious Reflections

In mirrors bright, reflections show,
The depths of life, the ebb and flow.
Each face a tale, a moment caught,
In every glance, a lesson taught.

The past and future intertwine,
In silent echoes, I define.
With every setback, every gain,
The journey's worth the joy and pain.

Together we learn from every scar,
Finding strength in who we are.
In unity, our spirits rise,
Harmonious dreams beneath the skies.

So let us share what we have learned,
In every page, our hearts are turned.
With open minds and open hearts,
We'll write the tale, play our parts.

In this reflection, I see the grace,
The beauty found in every space.
For as we gather, and as we mend,
In harmonious love, we transcend.

Fragments of Brilliance

In the whispers of dawn's light,
Shadows dance with gentle grace,
Each spark a fleeting insight,
Heartbeats echo in this space.

Colors burst in silent bloom,
Within the cracks of the old stone,
Dreams unfurl against the gloom,
In moments felt but not alone.

Glimmers rise from ashes past,
Each fragment a story told,
Threads of memories amassed,
In the tapestry of gold.

As night falls and silence reigns,
The stars remind us what was bright,
Each twinkle escapes the chains,
A spark of joy in dark's flight.

In the end, as all things fade,
What remains is love's embrace,
Though time and space have played,
We find solace in the grace.

Dazzling Echoes

Beneath the arch of twilight skies,
Whispers of the past resound,
In the laughter, softness lies,
Memories drift and spin around.

Colors merging, bright and bold,
An orchestra of light and sound,
Each echo a story retold,
In the heart where dreams are found.

Time stretches like a warm embrace,
Holding echoes of the day,
In the shadows, light finds space,
Chasing fragments on the way.

Dazzling lights begin to fade,
As stars awaken from their sleep,
Each whisper, a serenade,
In the silence, secrets keep.

Yet in this ever-spinning night,
Awake we stand, again refreshed,
For in the dark, we sense the light,
In dazzling echoes, we are blessed.

Glint of the Moon

Silver beams on waves collide,
A shimmer on the ocean's face,
In quiet moments, we confide,
With secrets in this timeless space.

Beneath the watchful, glowing eye,
Whispers linger in the air,
As night unfolds and dreams will fly,
In silver threads, we find our care.

The glint of hope in shadows cast,
A beacon through the forests deep,
In the silence, stillness lasts,
As visions come, but never leap.

The moon's caress, a soft embrace,
Reminds us of the love we seek,
Though time may wear a weary face,
In glimmers, truth remains unique.

As dawn approaches, light will rise,
Yet in the night, we hold the tune,
For every heart that learns to sigh,
Finds solace in the glint of the moon.

Spectrum of Silence

In the quiet of the night,
Colors blend in whispers soft,
Each shade a hidden insight,
A canvas where dreams lift aloft.

Silence speaks in vibrant tones,
A melody that plays within,
Where thoughts can dance on tender stones,
And shadows rise where lights have been.

Moments grasped, yet lightly held,
In echoes that softly fade away,
A spectrum where mysteries dwelled,
In twilight's grip, they gently sway.

Through stillness, beauty often grows,
Each breath a brushstroke in the dark,
In silence, a heart truly knows,
The quiet magic, a tender spark.

As dawn unfurls its golden wings,
The spectrum shifts, starts anew,
Yet still within our hearts, it clings,
This silence weaves the world in view.

Radiant Elysium

In fields where dreams do sway,
Bright blooms dance in the air.
Each whisper tells a tale,
Of souls that linger fair.

Beneath the azure skies,
Elysium softly glows.
With laughter in the breeze,
A harmony that flows.

Golden rays embrace the earth,
Where shadows dare not creep.
In light we find our mirth,
In joy, our hearts shall leap.

Each moment unfolds grace,
A sweet, unbroken spell.
In this enchanted place,
All wounds shall heal and swell.

Together we rejoice,
In this radiant domain.
With love, our hearts shall voice,
The beauty in our pain.

Luminous Horizons

Awake beneath the dawn,
Where sun and moon collide.
Horizons calling on,
With light as our guide.

Each step a journey bold,
Into the great unknown.
With stories yet untold,
Our dreams shall be sown.

Clouds painted in gold hues,
As day breaks through the night.
Unveiling vibrant views,
In the soft morning light.

From mountains to the seas,
The world begins to glow.
With every gentle breeze,
Our spirits start to flow.

We chase the endless skies,
With hope that never dims.
In luminous replies,
The universe begins.

Light's Melancholy

In shadows softly cast,
A flicker fades away.
Memories hold me fast,
In dreams I long to stay.

Each ray now bittersweet,
As twilight cloaks the day.
Beneath the sorrowed beat,
I find my heart's dismay.

The stars begin to sigh,
As night unfolds its veil.
A longing in the sky,
As echoes softly wail.

Yet in this dark embrace,
The light still tries to bloom.
Resilience finds its place,
Amidst the gathering gloom.

So let the shadows dance,
For every tear we shed.
In light's frail romance,
We find the path we tread.

Brightness of Solitude

In silence, I can hear,
The whispers of my soul.
Solitude is near,
Filling the empty bowl.

With every passing thought,
A glow begins to rise.
In stillness, I am taught,
To seek the vastest skies.

Each moment feels a gift,
A dance with my own heart.
In this sublime rift,
I weave my sacred art.

Alone, yet never lost,
In brightness, I am whole.
With every gentle cost,
I nurture my own role.

For in this quiet light,
I find my truest self.
Embracing every night,
As wealth beyond all wealth.

Reflective Reverie

In quiet moments, thoughts take flight,
Whispers of dreams dance in the night.
Each memory glimmers, softly bright,
   Guiding the heart to find its light.

Past shadows linger, softly sway,
   Carried by echoes of yesterday.
Each lesson learned, a gentle ray,
   Illuminates the winding way.

The mind drifts softly, like a stream,
Carving a path through the heart's dream.
Reflections linger, a silver gleam,
   In the silence, truths redeem.

Beneath the stars, thoughts intertwine,
   Lost in the magic of the divine.
Embracing the journey, life's design,
   In the reflective reverie, we shine.

Awakening whispers of the soul,
Each fleeting moment, a precious whole.
In the tapestry of time, we stroll,
Finding our essence, becoming whole.

Glint of Dawn

A gentle blush strokes the sky wide,
Awakening worlds, where shadows hide.
The horizon whispers, a hopeful guide,
In the glint of dawn, dreams abide.

Waves of gold dance on the sea,
Embracing the light, wild and free.
Morning blooms with pure glee,
As day breaks forth, a symphony.

Birds take flight, a joyous song,
Celebrating moments, righting the wrong.
In the hush of dawn, we all belong,
In nature's arms, forever strong.

Each soft glance, a promise new,
As sunrays kiss the morning dew.
We rise with hope, and spirits flew,
In the glint of dawn, our dreams renew.

Through the palette of day, colors blend,
In the heart of morning, we transcend.
With every heartbeat, paths extend,
To horizons bright, where fates mend.

Veils of Light

In twilight's whispers, secrets blend,
Veils of light, where shadows wend.
Illusions dance, and spirits send,
Messages tender, hearts to mend.

Luminescent dreams softly soar,
Through the night, to the ocean's floor.
Stars provide the guidance we adore,
In veils of light, we seek for more.

Glimmers shimmer on the face of time,
A melody of reason, rhythm, rhyme.
Life's mysteries unfold, purely sublime,
Wrapped in the glow of the divine.

In every corner, a tale ignites,
Caught in the softness of starry nights.
Hope resides in these glowing lights,
In veils of light, the heart ignites.

Awake to wonders, as day creeps in,
Where daylight breaks, let journeys begin.
Bound by the beauty of the within,
Veils of light lift, and spirits spin.

Spectrum's Embrace

Colors collide in a brilliant swirl,
A canvas alive, where dreams unfurl.
In the spectrum's embrace, possibilities twirl,
Painting the world with hope's soft pearl.

Gentle hues blush in the morning's breath,
Each shade a promise, defying death.
In the vibrant realms, we find our depth,
A symphony of life, a dance of heft.

Crimson whispers of love's embrace,
Golden laughter in every trace.
Emerald visions, a tender grace,
In spectrum's arms, we find our place.

Every pixel gleams with hidden light,
Transforming shadows into delight.
In the endless hues of day and night,
The spectrum's embrace makes futures bright.

Together we rise, hand in hand,
Creating a tapestry, woven and grand.
In each color, a story planned,
In spectrum's embrace, we take our stand.

Glistening Elysium

In fields where dreams take flight,
Where flowers bloom in golden light,
A stream of whispers, soft and clear,
Calls to the soul, drawing near.

The stars above, a radiant maze,
Guide our hearts through endless days,
With every step, the laughter grows,
In this paradise, love freely flows.

Mountains rise with a shimmering hue,
Each peak adorned with morning dew,
The air is sweet, a gentle kiss,
In Elysium, we find our bliss.

Moments stretch, like shadows cast,
In this realm, time drifts so fast,
Yet in its grasp, we hold our peace,
In glistening realms, our worries cease.

Afterglow of Hope

As twilight fades to soft embrace,
The sun departs, but leaves a trace,
A golden glow that warms the chill,
Awakens dreams, ignites the will.

With every star that starts to rise,
A promise twinkles in the skies,
Guiding hearts that seek to mend,
In every shadow, light descend.

The dusk unfolds, a canvas bright,
Where every color battles night,
In whispers soft, the world ignites,
A symphony of endless sights.

Together, we watch the heavens blend,
Finding solace, hand in hand,
In the afterglow, we dare to cope,
For in the night, there lies our hope.

Shards of Infinity

In every moment, time does break,
Fragments spark, like ripples wake,
A dance of echoes, sharp and clear,
In the void, our path appears.

Through realms unseen, we chase the light,
Shards of truth in endless flight,
Weaving dreams through cosmic threads,
As the universe quietly spreads.

With every breath, the chaos swirls,
In spirals bright, our fate unfurls,
The tapestry of life expands,
In unity, we join our hands.

In infinite ways, we choose to grow,
As stars collide in cosmic flow,
Among the shards, our spirits soar,
Discovering worlds, unlocking doors.

Dazzle in the Dark

In velvet night, where shadows creep,
The stars awake, secrets to keep,
A dance of light on wings of fate,
Unraveling dreams, we contemplate.

With every twinkle, tales are spun,
Of distant worlds, of joys begun,
In silence, we hear the cosmos sing,
A melody of hope we bring.

Through paths unknown, our hearts align,
In the darkness, we see the shine,
With every step, we find our way,
A dazzle bright to light the gray.

Embracing fears, we rise anew,
In luminous echoes, stars break through,
For in the dark, we learn to spark,
The magic of a vibrant arc.

Luminous Tides

The waves embrace the shore so bright,
Glimmers dance in soft moonlight.
Each whisper carries tales untold,
In depths of blue, secrets unfold.

The sun dips low, a golden hue,
Brushes the sea, a vibrant view.
Stars awaken, their song begins,
The ocean breathes, where silence spins.

In tides that swell, dreams take flight,
Hearts converge beneath the night.
With every ebb, new hopes arise,
Reflecting worlds in endless skies.

The rising swell, like pulse of life,
Bears witness to our joy and strife.
Each crest a promise, each trough a fall,
In luminous tides, we find it all.

Shining Truths

In shadows cast, truth finds its glow,
A beacon bright through doors of woe.
Every heart bears its hidden flame,
Illuminates the lost, the same.

Through whispered words and gentle hands,
We grasp the light and make our stands.
In laughter shared, in tears released,
The shining truths are worth the feast.

A canvas painted with shades of grace,
Revealing love in every space.
With every smile, a story breathes,
In shining truths, the soul believes.

No longer blind, we choose to see,
Those hidden gems in you and me.
Embrace the light that warms our days,
In shining truths, our spirits blaze.

Brilliance Beneath

Beyond the surface, the depths lie still,
A treasure trove, a hidden thrill.
With grains of sand and whispers low,
Brilliance beneath, in currents flow.

The ocean's heart, a silent call,
Holds tales of rise, embraces fall.
Shadows dance with sunlight's kiss,
In every wave, a glimpse of bliss.

Like hidden dreams in moonlit tides,
Beliefs unfold where courage abides.
What's lost in dark will find its way,
In brilliance beneath, night turns to day.

The calm unveils the tempest's might,
Soft glimmers spark the endless night.
From depths of fear, new visions glean,
Brilliance beneath, forever seen.

Veil of Illumination

A soft veil drapes the twilight sky,
Hiding wonders, as stars draw nigh.
Through gentle whispers, light takes form,
In chaos calm, a peaceful storm.

Each dawn reveals a canvas bright,
With strokes of gold and hues of light.
Underneath the veil, dreams wake,
In every moment, chances take.

A dance of shadows, a play of truth,
The veil reveals the heart of youth.
Through laughter shared and lives entwined,
In veil of illumination, love's defined.

Each fleeting glance, a spark ignites,
A journey bound in endless flights.
Beneath the veil, we find our place,
In illumination, we embrace.

Prisms of Light

Fragments of color dance in the air,
Shifting and swirling, a vibrant flare.
Sunlight refracted through windows so clear,
Creating a spectrum, a world we hold dear.

Glistening beams paint the walls with delight,
Mirroring dreams that enchant through the night.
Each hue a whisper, soft and so bright,
In the heart of the moment, we bask in their light.

Crimson and sapphire, gold's warm embrace,
Chasing the shadows that fell from their grace.
Nature's own canvas, a vibrant showcase,
Prisms of wonder, in time we will trace.

When twilight descends, and the sun starts to wane,
The colors will linger, yet never in vain.
A tapestry woven, in joy and in pain,
Prisms of light shall forever remain.

So look for the beauty in moments we share,
In prisms of light that dance through the air.
For life is ephemeral, fleeting and rare,
Yet boundless and bright, if we just dare to care.

Ethereal Dusk

Whispers of twilight embrace the still night,
Drawing the stars with a gentle invite.
Shadows now linger, soft folds of the dark,
Painting the heavens, a mystical arc.

Crescent moon hanging like a pendant of pearl,
Casting a glow that begins to unfurl.
The night winds are carrying tales from afar,
While silence awakens dreams under the star.

Veils of soft mist wrap the earth in their light,
Merging the shadows in elegance, bright.
A world interwoven in peace and in grace,
Ethereal dusk holds us in its embrace.

Time flows like water through fingers of bliss,
Moments like whispers, a fleeting caress.
In the arms of the night, where secrets reside,
Ethereal dusk keeps our dreams as a guide.

So let us wander where soft fancies bloom,
Beneath the vast cloak that dispels all the gloom.
For in this soft twilight, we gently find rest,
Ethereal dusk cradles all of our best.

Luminous Echoes

Voices of ages ripple through the night,
Casting reflections in the soft silver light.
Each whisper a tale of the dreams that were spun,
Luminous echoes of laughter and fun.

Time resonates softly like whispers of lace,
Moments entwined in a delicate space.
Fleeting and fragile, yet full of delight,
In luminous echoes, the heart takes its flight.

Gentle reminders of journeys we've made,
Footsteps in shadows, memories won't fade.
Like flickering lanterns, they beckon and call,
Luminous echoes, the stories of all.

Connect us together, the past and the now,
In shimmering harmony, life takes a bow.
For in every echo, we find who we are,
Luminous treasures, a guiding bright star.

So cherish the whispers that dance on the air,
For echoes of beauty are precious and rare.
With each passing moment, let your spirit rise,
Luminous echoes, a gift in disguise.

Woven in Shine

Threads of existence entwined in a glow,
Gathered together through high and through low.
Each moment a fiber, they sparkle and gleam,
Woven in shine, we illuminate dreams.

Gentle connections, we weave with our hearts,
Tangled serendipity, where each frame starts.
Bonds that reflect in the light of the sun,
Woven in shine, where our journeys are spun.

Colors of laughter, the hues of our tears,
Crafted in shining, our hopes and our fears.
A tapestry rich with the tales we hold tight,
Woven in shine, we embrace the pure light.

With every encounter, a stitch in the weave,
Creating a quilt of what we can believe.
In unity's warmth, we rise and define,
Woven in shine, a legacy fine.

So cherish the fibers that tie us as one,
Through beauty and struggle, our spirits have spun.
For in every thread, a connection divine,
Woven in shine, our stories entwined.

Twilight Glimmer

The day fades softly into night,
Bathed in hues of gentle light.
Stars awaken, shimmering bright,
Guiding dreams in their flight.

Whispers of dusk in the air,
A tranquil moment, oh so rare.
Nature bows without a care,
Embracing peace beyond compare.

The horizon blushes with grace,
As shadows dance, a slow embrace.
In twilight's glow, we find our place,
A fleeting, magical space.

Time stands still in this embrace,
Moments linger, love's sweet trace.
As night unfolds in soft pace,
We cherish each starry face.

In twilight glimmer, hearts ignite,
A symphony of pure delight.
We gather dreams in the night,
As hope takes wing, taking flight.

Ghost of Light

In shadows deep, where echoes sigh,
A ghost of light begins to fly.
It weaves through dreams, a fleeting high,
Illuminating truths we deny.

A whispering glow on troubled seas,
Tales of wonder, lost at ease.
It calls to hearts, a gentle tease,
Awakening warmth like summer's breeze.

These flickers dance with haunting grace,
A fleeting glimpse, a soft embrace.
In every soul, it finds a place,
Revealing love's eternal trace.

Yet time moves on, the light may fade,
But memories linger, never betrayed.
In darkness found, a path is laid,
By every joy and pain we made.

So hold the ghost, embrace its flight,
For in its glow, you'll find your light.
With every heartbeat, bold and bright,
We carry on through endless night.

Shimmering Solitude

In silent woods, a stillness calls,
Where nature's grace within me sprawls.
A soft retreat as twilight falls,
In shimmering solitude, truth installs.

The rustling leaves, a whispered sigh,
Beneath the vast and starry sky.
In solitude, where dreams can lie,
I find a self, no need to try.

Each moment lingers, rich and deep,
Where gentle shadows softly creep.
In this embrace, my spirit leaps,
A treasure found in peace I keep.

Time flows slow in this sacred space,
With every heartbeat, I find grace.
In shimmering hues, I leave a trace,
Of silent joy, life's softest face.

So here I dwell, where stillness hums,
In solitude's heart, my spirit comes.
A world apart, where peace becomes,
The solace sought, as silence drums.

Brilliance of the Unseen

In quiet corners, wonders gleam,
Beyond the veil, where hearts may dream.
The brilliance of the unseen stream,
Awakens hope, a radiant beam.

In shadows cast, a spark ignites,
A dance of souls in secret nights.
Invisible threads weave our delights,
Holding close what love unites.

Amidst the chaos, wisdom flows,
In whispered truths that softly grows.
Beneath the surface, feeling glows,
A brilliance born from what one knows.

Time's gentle grace weaves tales untold,
In every heart, a fire bold.
The unseen beauty, rich as gold,
Binds us together, manifold.

So trust the light that's yet to be,
In every shadow, find the key.
For in the dark, we learn to see,
The brilliance of our destiny.

Glistening Memories

In the quiet shadows we roam,
Treasures of laughter, a place called home.
Whispers of ages, soft as a sigh,
Glistening moments that never say goodbye.

Fleeting like sunlight on dew-kissed ground,
Echoes of joy in each heartbeat found.
Stories entwined in the fabric of time,
Each thread a memory, a delicate rhyme.

Through wisps of clouds, our dreams take flight,
Painting the canvas of velvet night.
With stars as our guide, we journey afar,
Chasing the glow of our own northern star.

Time may fade, but the feelings remain,
Captured in moments, transcending the pain.
Glistening memories, forever preserved,
A treasure chest of love, so richly deserved.

With heartstrings tethered to places unknown,
We carve out the pathways where warmth has grown.
In laughter and tears, we find our way,
In glistening memories, forever we stay.

Pearls in the Night

Under the blanket where shadows rest,
We gather dreams, already blessed.
Each twinkle a tale, each star a wish,
Pearls in the night, the heart's sweetest dish.

Moonlight dances upon the calm sea,
Mysteries whisper, oh let them be.
Gentle reflections on water's face,
In the quiet night, we find our place.

With every breath, the world seems to pause,
Beneath the darkness, we find our cause.
In the silence, our spirits ignite,
Chasing the pearls hidden in the night.

Stories unfold in a tapestry grand,
Woven of dreams held in time's gentle hand.
Boundless horizons where wishes take flight,
Together we shine, oh pearls in the night.

In the stillness, our hearts intertwine,
Lost in the beauty, forever divine.
Each moment a jewel, each glance a delight,
We treasure the magic, the pearls in the night.

Opalescent Visions

In a world kissed by the dawn's soft light,
Colors collide, a beautiful sight.
Dreams unfold like petals in bloom,
Opalescent visions dispel the gloom.

Rays of the sun dance on leaves and stone,
Whispering secrets in soft undertones.
Ethereal glow that warms the heart,
In opalescent visions, we play our part.

Each flicker of hope casts shadows away,
Guiding us gently through night into day.
With every sunrise, the canvas grows bright,
Opalescent visions ignite our flight.

Infinite wonder in nature's embrace,
We chase the colors, a thrilling race.
Inspiration flows like a river of light,
Through opalescent visions, we take our height.

As twilight descends, the hues softly blend,
A masterpiece crafted, no need to pretend.
With wonder and grace, we meet the new night,
In opalescent visions, our spirits take flight.

Shards of Beauty

Fragments of light, scattered and bright,
Shards of beauty, a breathtaking sight.
Crystals of laughter, echoes of cheer,
In this mosaic, our hearts draw near.

Through trials and storms, we find our way,
Each shard a reminder, come what may.
Reflections of strength in the face of despair,
In shards of beauty, we find love to share.

Colors collide in a dance so divine,
A tapestry woven, our lives intertwine.
In moments of grace, we learn to forgive,
Embracing the shards that teach us to live.

With courage we gather the pieces we find,
Reclaiming the past, and the ties that bind.
Each sparkle a memory, a lesson from fate,
In shards of beauty, we navigate.

So let us celebrate the colors we see,
In life's shattered lens, it's clear we're free.
With hearts wide open, we'll weather the storm,
In shards of beauty, our souls are reborn.

Shimmering Essence

In twilight's embrace, whispers unfold,
A dance of shadows, secrets retold.
Glimmers of starlight, soft as a sigh,
A tapestry woven in the night sky.

Where silence echoes, dreams begin flight,
With each gentle pulse, hearts feel the light.
Ethereal laughter, carried on breeze,
Under the canopy of ancient trees.

In puddles of silver, reflections collide,
The essence of magic, flows like the tide.
Fleeting moments, a cherished embrace,
In shimmering depths, we find our place.

With whispers of hope, we rise and we fall,
The shimmering essence, binds us in thrall.
A serenade sung, in luminous tones,
Connecting our spirits, sewing our bones.

So let us rejoice, in this glittering sphere,
For in shimmering essence, love conquers fear.
The cosmos aligns, in swirling delight,
Together we shine, our souls take flight.

Translucent Dreams

Drifting through realms where the colors blend,
In translucent dreams, time has no end.
Waves of soft whispers, brush past the ear,
A symphony's echo, that's heartfelt and clear.

Each thought a petal, floating on air,
Carried by breezes, without a care.
A canvas invisible, painted by night,
As laughter and wishes dance in the light.

In visions of wonder, we wander and trace,
A world made of fabric, both fragile and grace.
Embracing the shadows that play in the dark,
With every heartbeat, we leave our mark.

The melody swells, in colors so bright,
Translucent dreams weave, magic in flight.
With wings made of stardust, we soar and we glide,
Through the paths of our minds, where all dreams reside.

So close your eyes gently, let visions arise,
In translucent dreams, we're free to be wise.
The universe whispers, in hues so divine,
Embracing our spirits, two hearts intertwine.

Prismatic Light

In prisms of color, the world comes alive,
Each ray a reminder, of how we thrive.
Through laughter and joy, we scatter the night,
Embracing the dance of prismatic light.

A kaleidoscope view, where moments collide,
Every fragment a story, no need to hide.
With brushes of sunshine, painting the air,
In prismatic hues, we banish despair.

The whispers of dawn, spread warmth on our skin,
Each beam's gentle touch, invites us to begin.
Feel the pulse of the universe, vibrant and grand,
While colors awaken, as we take a stand.

In unity's bloom, we rise with the day,
In prismatic light, we find our own way.
Bound by the spectrum, together we rise,
Beneath painted skies, we'll always surprise.

So turn towards the glow, and let it ignite,
In every heart's corner, lives prismatic light.
A tapestry woven in hues ever bold,
Together we shine, a story retold.

Celestial Sparkle

In the quiet of night, stars start to sing,
A celestial sparkle, the cosmos brings.
With wishes igniting, like fireflies dance,
Each glimmer a promise, a timeless chance.

From constellations, stories unfold,
In vastness of space, with wonders untold.
The universe whispers, with shimmering grace,
In celestial sparkle, we find our place.

Galaxies twinkle, in depths of the sky,
A tapestry woven, where dreams learn to fly.
The fabric of night, adorned with pure light,
Inviting our hearts to sparkle so bright.

Infinite visions, a dance of the spheres,
Every twinkle a heartbeat, beyond all our fears.
Within stardust realms, we align and create,
In celestial sparkle, we celebrate fate.

So gaze at the heavens, let wonder ignite,
For in every twinkle, shines infinite light.
Hand in hand with the cosmos, let's journey afar,
In the glow of the night, we're each a bright star.